G000134344

ot a Boy Soldier

A Great War Memoir
By George Parker

Telling the tales of Brighton & Hove

Acknowledgements

Published by QueenSpark Books, Community Publishers
QueenSpark is a not for profit organisation committed to offering
affordable public access to writing and publishing. All profits made on
our books and stationery go back into funding our work.

QueenSpark Books
Room 211, 10 – 11 Pavilion Parade, Brighton BN2 1RA
Telephone: 01273 571710
www.queensparkbooks.org.uk
www.thedeckchair.org.uk

© Copyright QueenSpark Books 2008
ISBN: 9-780904-733-433
A catalogue of this book is available at the British Library.

For this 2008 Edition

Managing Editor: Sarah Hutchings
Editor: Anne Morrison
Cover Design: Jesse Green
Design and typesetting: Stella Cardus, Desktop Display
We would like to thank the following people who have been generous
with their assistance during the making of this book: Rosemary Allix,
Jo Legg, Anthony Richards of the Imperial War Museum, Tom
Sawyer at the University of Brighton BA(Hons) Graphic Design and
Chris Trueman.
All pictures of George Parker appear courtesy of the Imperial War
Museum © (these were originally donated by George Parker's
daughter, the late Pat Brown). Other images are credited throughout.

For the 2001 Edition

This book was made by June Martin, Pamela Platt and Krista
Woodley. We would also like to thank David Beevers, Keeper of
Preston Manor, Brighton; Jack Berwitz, Keith Hood and Jools Poore
for proof reading; Steven Broomfield, Chairman of the Hampshire and
Isle of Wight branch of The Western Front Association; Mrs Pat
Brown; Dr Kate Harris, Librarian and Archivist to the Marquess of
Bath; Local Studies Library, Brighton; Sheena Macdonald; Bob Platt
and Anthony Richards of the Imperial War Museum.

Prologue

In 1999, QueenSpark Books received a manuscript written by George Parker. Entitled by him "G.K. Parker - History and Memories", it describes his boyhood in Brighton in the early 1900s, and his service as a 15 year old volunteer soldier in the First World War.

Although George Parker completed the manuscript around 1969, it did not come to light until a few days after his death in 1973 when his daughter, Mrs Pat Brown, found it among his belongings. He had not spoken to her about his often traumatic experiences in the First World War, nor had he mentioned the vividly descriptive manuscript that he had written. It was initially read out in public at the monthly meetings of the Hampshire and Isle of Wight branch of The Western Front Association, of which Mrs Brown was a member.

We are grateful to Mrs Brown for sending the manuscript to QueenSpark Books and are proud to publish this fascinating life history. We have made only minor editorial amendments to the manuscript. All dates, place names and buildings mentioned here are George's recollections; events do not always appear in chronological order, buildings mentioned in the text may no longer exist, and place names may have changed.

Foreword

'Your King and Country Need You' declared a popular recruiting poster issued immediately after the outbreak of the First World War in August 1914. Among the requirements for Army service were that the man in question should be 5ft 3 inches or upward in height, medically fit and measuring 34 inches around the chest, and be aged between 19 and 30.

Immediately we see the relevance of the title of George Parker's memoir. The common desire to 'do their bit' for their country impelled many young men to lie about their true age in order to be accepted into the Army, and in this respect George was by no means unique in enlisting at the age of 15. Indeed, his subsequent experiences of the war were not so different to those of many of his contemporaries: an initial enthusiasm ultimately tainted by the harsh reality of trench warfare.

This memoir of service on the Western Front forms exactly the kind of personal war record that we are keen to preserve in the archive of the Imperial War Museum. The Museum's ever-expanding holdings of British and Commonwealth personal papers now amount to over 16,000 unique collections of letters, diaries and memoirs. As part of the national collection, all are available for individuals to consult and remain a crucial historical source for researchers worldwide, ranging from schoolchildren studying A-levels through to academics completing their theses.

George Parker's original typescript and photographs are now permanently preserved in the Museum's Department of Documents, where future generations will be able to make full use of this valuable first-hand account.

Anthony Richards
Archivist, Imperial War Museum

Timeline of World War One

1914

June 28	Francis Ferdinand assassinated in Sarajevo
July 5	Kaiser William II promised German support for Austria against Serbia
July 28	Austria declared war on Serbia
August 1	Germany declared war on Russia
August 3	Germany declared war on France and invaded Belgium
August 4	Britain declared war on Germany
August 23	The British Expeditionary Force started its retreat from Mons
	Germany invaded France
August 26	Russian army defeated at Tannenburg and Masurian Lakes
September 6	Battle of the Marne started
October 18	First Battle of Ypres
October 29	Turkey entered the war on Germany's side
	Trench warfare started to dominate the Western Front

1915

January 19	The first Zeppelin raid on Britain
February 19	Britain bombarded Turkish forts in the Dardanelles
April 25	Allied troops landed in Gallipoli
May 7	"Lusitania" was sunk by a German U-boat
May 23	Italy declared war on Germany and Austria
August 5	The Germans captured Warsaw from the Russians
September 25	Start of the Battle of Loos
December 19	Allies started the evacuation of Gallipoli

1916

January 27	Conscription introduced in Britain
February 21	Start of the Battle of Verdun
April 29	British forces surrendered to Turkish forces at Kut in Mesopotamia
May 31	Battle of Jutland
July 1	Start of the Battle of the Somme
September 15	First use en masse of tanks at the Somme
December 7	Lloyd George became British Prime Minister

1917

February 1	Germany's unrestricted submarine warfare campaign started
April 6	USA declared war on Germany
April 16	France launched an unsuccessful offensive on the Western Front
July 31	Start of the Third Battle at Ypres
October 24	Battle of Caporetto – the Italian Army heavily defeated
November 6	Britain launched a major offensive on the Western Front
November 20	British tanks won a victory at Cambrai
December 5	Armistice between Germany and Russia
December 9	Britain captured Jerusalem from the Turks

1918

March 3	The Treaty of Brest-Litovsk was signed between Russia and Germany
March 21	Germany broke through on the Somme
March 29	Marshall Foch was appointed Allied Commander on the Western Front
April 9	Germany started an offensive in Flanders
July 15	Second Battle of the Marne Start of the collapse of the German army
August 8	The advance of the Allies was successful
September 19	Turkish forces collapsed at Megiddo
October 4	Germany asked the Allies for an armistice
October 29	Germany's navy mutinied
October 30	Turkey made peace
November 3	Austria made peace
November 9	Kaiser William II abdicated
November 11	Germany signed an armistice with the Allies

Extract taken from WW1 timeline on www.historylearningsite.co.uk

Courtesy of Chris Trueman

H. T. Edwards,

The Grove,
Electric Light Studio,
10, Lewes Road,
Brighton.

George Parker 1898-1973

Growing up in Brighton

I was born on Saturday 10th September 1898 at 49 Southampton Street, Brighton, Sussex, the third child of Edwin Ernest Parker and Charlotte Grace Parker, nee Purser. Their first child, a girl named Emma Rosina, was born in 1893, and their second child, Ernest Edwin, was born in 1896 but died aged nine months old. Albert Edward and Frederick were born in 1902 and 1907 respectively, while Grace Alice was the last to be born in 1909.

My father was apprenticed to a tailor in Boyces Street, Brighton. I am not quite clear where he first met my mother but I know that when he and my mother were married he was hardly out of his apprenticeship and so had not managed to get a trade connection together. When the first three children had arrived they were in great poverty. Apart from financial worries, there was the search for a suitable place where Dad could carry out his work. They must have wandered the town searching for a place, poor devils, for we lived in many different parts of the town, among them: Kemp Street, London Terrace, Hanover Street, Lincoln Street and Southover Street. By the time I was about six years of age we were living at 51 Southover Street. At first we lived in rooms with Mum's aunt, Anne Dempsey, who ran a hand laundry at 52 Southover Street. Then, as the family increased and number 51 became vacant, we moved there.

My Dad was not one who made it easy to get close to him. He seemed shy of showing his feelings; children sense that and tend to draw away. He was good, kind and, like Mum, sacrificed a lot for us kids but, being a strict disciplinarian, it seemed as though I mainly looked to him for tannings. He had had a very hard childhood and that, as well as being crippled for most of his life, did not help. I now know how frustrating it is to be crippled but I didn't at that time. Dad had lost his left leg when only ten years of age through neglect on the part of his mother after he came home with a damaged knee as a result of a fall while playing leapfrog outside his school in Southover Street. She treated it as of no importance but it turned septic and, after months of hospital treatment, the leg was amputated. Ten years of age and crippled for life.

Gran Parker was formerly a Hounsel, a family who originally came from Cosham in Hampshire. She was a real tough country woman of the old school, no softness but plenty of strict Baptist Church and spankings. Her kids had a very rough passage through childhood. Gran Parker was a hardworking, house-proud woman who would scrub all the paint off everything and then tell the landlord that it wanted doing up. When my sister and I went to see her - a duty call, I'm afraid - the first we heard was her shout of "Wipe your boots!". In fact, on one occasion, Dad's sister slipped on the front door mat, polished underneath, and slid right along the passage. Being a strict Baptist of course I suppose she just said "Bust it", or some other four-letter word! To my mind, Gran was a Dickensian type of parent. Children were not to be heard, and not to be seen either. She and her husband had parted years before I was old enough to know. He was the general foreman of a building firm and had a hand in building a number of big places in the district, among them St. Bartholomew's Church and the Police Convalescent Home in Hove.

My other grandmother, Mum's mother, lived in a picturesque cottage in Withdean, near Preston village just outside Brighton. Her husband, Thomas Purser, was an architect but had died when barely out of his initial training, leaving her poor and with two young children. They lived in Latchmere Road, off Lavender Hill, in Battersea, London, but, having relatives in the Brighton area, she moved there. By the time I was old enough to know, she had married the head gardener at Lady Ogle's big house at Withdean, now, alas, all gone and built over. Step-grandad was a cheerful, bearded man, always full of fun with my elder sister and myself. Consequently we both loved him. Gran herself was a warm, affectionate woman, like our Mum. Together, they were the two people I most loved as a kid and, after all these years, I still feel the same about them.

Schooldays

When I first started school we were living in Kemp Street (off Trafalgar Street) and went to the old Pelham Street School, now rebuilt. My teacher was a Miss Flint and she was aptly named. All of us small kids were scared to death of her and she really enjoyed that. We seemed to spend such a long time at prayers; kneeling on the hard, bare boards while 'Flinty' read out seemingly endless prayers so that our poor little bony knees ached furiously. This teacher had a deep-rooted objection to any pupil going to the toilet. Of course, the inevitable happened. One day, after being refused, I could not wait and had an accident in my knickers. I did not dare to say anything so was forced to remain in that state until we were released to go home for dinner. I well remember, small as I was, how I crept into the house and out to the lavatory which in those days was right at the bottom of the garden, and tried to clean myself up. I was a sensitive sort of kid and did not want my Mum to know, as though she wouldn't find out anyway. Queer things, kids!

Once we moved to Southover Street, I attended Finsbury Road School whose entrance was next door to my house, although when a boiler blew up, us infants had to go to a temporary school at Bentham Road Mission Hall, now Bentham Road Church[1]. I started there with another small boy, Walter Barnes aged four or five, who, for some unknown reason, we kids nicknamed 'Jumbo'. This boy was my pal until I lost sight of him after the First World War. Ships that pass in the night. When the Finsbury Road School reopened and we returned there, I soon found that I could climb over our garden wall into the playground. Owing to that, I was able to be the first in the playground before the gate was opened.

In school at that time, tanning was a regular thing. After a serious offence, a few of the masters were in the habit of making a boy lay across the master's desk and then they really laid it on. One master made a boy take down his knickers first. Of course, it would not be allowed now; they have gone to the other extreme.

During my later years at school I was a member of the choir chosen to represent the school at the Empire Singing Festival held at the Crystal Palace, near Penge in London. This was a wonderful experience; thousands of boys and girls singing their hearts out. It was a thrill to take part, but it must have sounded even better to the audience in the auditorium and galleries. There was a great organ high up at the back and tiers of seats in front and below filled with

---

[1] Bentham Road Church closed in the 1980s.

children singing for the honour of their various schools. We were proud of our schools then. In some cases this pride has died out and it is not always the fault of the kids.

Starting work

At the age of nine, in between school hours, I started work at a grocer's shop opposite my home. Named the Up-to-Date Stores, on the corner of Quebec Street and Southover Street, it was kept by a Mr Evelyn Powell and his wife. They had a daughter, Doris, a little dark-haired kid of my own age, with large brown eyes. I, at nine years of age, fell in love with her at first sight. Life is funny - I hardly knew the difference in the sexes then. They were a nice couple but of course couldn't pay very well. I received the princely sum of two shillings and sixpence per week working for an hour in the morning before school, a short time at dinner-time, and whatever time they needed me in the evenings. My Mum had two shillings and I had sixpence. I was quite happy about it as even that small amount helped the family coffers and most other kids were doing the same sort of thing working for butchers, grocers, greengrocers, dairymen and chemists. Every tradesman had a 'boy'. The morning work, 7.30 - 8.30, was spent doing jobs like sweeping out the shop and cleaning the windows. The floor of the shop was sprinkled with clean sawdust in the morning as was the custom in grocers, butchers and some other trades at that time. I used to take a two-wheeled trolley all the way to a sawmill in Ann Street to get a large sack of sawdust when it ran out.

I didn't have a carrier bike and I used to carry baskets of groceries as big as myself to houses in a wide area. In those days it was a case of leaning over to one side to take the load on your hip. However, I was not the only boy doing it; it was usual in poor families then and taken for granted by the kids. There were one or two carrier bikes about, but my boss could not afford one.

After a short time, I was shown how to weigh up sugar, soda and various other commodities. Everything came in loose at that time including tea which was blended specially for customers who wished it. On a long shelf, part of the fixtures behind the counter was a row of large, round canisters. These were often green and decorated with a golden dragon. They were numbered from one to ten, or more. Each one held a different tea: India, China, Pekoe and so on. When we were asked for a certain blend, a large sheet of paper was spread on the counter and, according to which blend the customer wanted, tea was weighed out of the canisters using a small brass scoop which, incidentally, I had to polish every day. Some of each required blend was weighed and put on the paper. Blending was done with the tips of the fingers by a lifting and stirring motion. Wrapping was in a rectangular piece of paper, usually with the grocer's name in a scroll design printed on it. Wrapping 'flat' with a commodity that moves and slides about takes some getting used to. Rice was the worst one but, once mastered, did not run out when wrapped. Most people were particular over the things they purchased then - not just a thing with a pretty label. In my opinion, there is more pleasure in serving a person who is particular and means to get just what she or he wants, than serving one who will be satisfied with anything.

I stayed with the Powells until I left school, by that time earning five shillings a week, but as Mr and Mrs Powell could not afford to pay more and my people were hard-up, I had to look out for another job. I then heard through the errand-boys' telegraph that a junior was wanted at E.C. Evershed's Supply Stores, at the top of Egremont Place, Queen's Park, so I went up there, saw the manager, Mr Wren, and got the job at 18 bob a week. I was a millionaire! I was very happy there, the manager being a good sort. I learned tea-blending and coffee-blending, cutting the various parts of a side of bacon, and many other facets of business in a high-class grocers, provisions and wine and spirit stores. I have no doubt that I received a good grounding for later years in the trade.

The staff were nice to work with too and had great patience with a juvenile who had a great deal to learn. Soon after starting there, I went to get a bottle of whisky from a rather high shelf and knocked one over. That one knocked another and soon there were a dozen assorted bottles of whisky and brandy smashed on the floor. My heart was in my mouth. I visualised at least being shot at dawn. The fumes were so strong, I was practically drunk. The value was considerable, even then: twelve and six per full-size bottle, and if I were to pay for the damage it would take my 18 bob wages for years. I was almost in tears and I think they were sorry for me; anyway, between them, they made it right with the stock sheets. Yes, they were good fellows - the best. I hope that some like them still exist today.

One of them committed suicide when he was out of work during the bad depression in the 1920s by jumping over the hundred foot cliff at Black Rock. The poor devil had just lost his wife too. One of the others died of tuberculosis. The manager lived to middle age. Like many others, the shop closed down in the early 1920s, owing to competition.

I stayed with Eversheds for some time until I heard that the Co-op wanted juniors and, as Eversheds could not run to another senior assistant and I wanted more money, I got a job there. It was a pity really as, of course, there was nothing high class about the Co-op. It was regarded as a step down to leave a good-class shop for a place like that. But I was young and the young seldom see far ahead. Also, my people were still hard-up so I had to get more money.

The Laundry

Although my father was doing a little better by now, two more children, Albert and Frederick, had arrived in the meantime. Oh, why don't adults think ahead, as they tell us to do? They had a hard struggle as it was, with Dad's business still small. However now there were four of us and only Dad and myself earning, so Mum went in with my Great Aunt Dempsey next door (she must have been in her seventies even then), to help her run the hand laundry which did quite well. People were more particular in those days and liked the hand-done, personal touch on their things. The work was done in the back basement room, and marvellous work those places turned out too. Every article was hand-washed and ironed and there were no detergents or bleaching powders used; customers wouldn't have put up with that anyway.

The only machine used was the box mangle, which dominated the room: a huge contraption like a very big wardrobe cupboard, about eight to ten feet long, laying horizontally on its back full of large beach boulders. This great weight was supported on wooden rollers each about ten inches in diameter. The semi-dry sheets and other large articles were laid flat on the bed of the mangle, a large wheel was turned by hand and the weight ran over the articles leaving them as smooth as if they had been ironed. I still remember the click of the 'dogs' (pieces of steel) which engaged each time the machine reversed.

The mangle was worked originally by Charlie Humphrey but by this time he had gone to work at Peter's Furniture Store in Kensington Gardens, where he stayed for 40 years. Charlie, by the way, was courting my Mum's sister, Annie. They courted for over 20 years before marrying. The mangle man now was Joe Patching, a totally blind, middle-aged man. He was marvellously clean and used to scrub the lower stairs and front stone steps until they were literally white - no corners left dirty, either! We kids were brought up to call Joe 'Uncle'. He was a very strict man with kids, but just I think. He died in about 1912 in the act of putting on his slippers and was found by Aunt sitting on the edge of his bed. His life-savings were found in a cupboard in his room, not much, but each pounds' worth of silver was carefully wrapped in a roll of newspaper and screwed round at the ends.

As often happens, he had heard nothing of any relatives for years, but they soon heard of his death and came to gather up the old chap's savings. Aunt never heard of them again. While on the subject of Joe, I remember that to augment his small income he had worked up a connection supplying Ship brand matches to pubs in Brighton and would travel all over the town just relying on his instinct and his stick on the kerb. What marvellous courage and determination he had!

Hard times

My parents displayed similar courage in the early days. Their second child, Ernest Edwin, had died of bronchial pneumonia in the Alexandra Children's Hospital on Dyke Road in Brighton. At the last he had terrible skin trouble and his little hands had to be tied to prevent scratching; poor little devil. Maybe it was caused by lack of proper nourishment for the mother - who knows? At least things are better in that way now; in fact things have gone to the other extreme. All I had as a kid was the usual whooping cough, measles and, worst of all, bilious attacks. How ill I was with those! My mother used to suffer with them too, so understood how I felt.

At the time that my brother Albert was born, the poverty was extreme. How Mum fed us, I can't imagine. I know that she filled us as much as possible with plain puddings that had jam or treacle on, and an occasional bread pudding. Christmas pudding was bread pudding with perhaps a little more fruit than usual and yet, with all that, Mum would send Emmie and I round to some relations in Agnes Street with a pudding and odd things because the husband was out of work. I well remember going there: practically no furniture, two small children crawling on the floor and one on the only bed.

It must be remembered that there was no unemployment pay then. One could only apply for Parish Relief; a very degrading thing, if one had any pride. A ticket would be issued only if you could prove that you were really destitute. This was a slip of paper with a few absolute necessities printed on it and the shops were forbidden to supply anything that was not on the list. The amount varied, but was mostly under ten shillings. I had poor women come in to the shop and beg me to let them have a little tobacco for their husbands instead of sugar (she would do without it in her tea), only her man had not had a smoke for so long. What could I do? I knew what poverty was so I would break the rules and let them have it. Yes, those were Dickensian days all right. The Parish also had soup kitchens in Cobden Road, where the very poor could get soup for tuppence a quart. I went there many times with a washstand jug to get a gallon for our dinner. It cost eightpence. It was quite good soup, or seemed like it to us, who were hungry.

The London Road Congregational Church had a 'blanket society' which would lend out blankets to the poor for the winter for a very small sum provided they were returned clean at the end. Emmie and I used to go for some blankets each winter to a Mr Hamilton in Wellington Road. The younger members of my family don't know of those hard times as Dad was more prosperous by the time they were old enough to understand. Maybe they would have had more thought for us older ones now, if they did. Mind you, we were not sorry for ourselves. A lot of families were in a like position. My main thought is of the worry and sacrifice that my parents, and other parents, had to suffer. How they fed and reared children, often in large numbers, beats me.

I remember one occasion when Mum was very hard-up. She sent me to the greengrocers for what she called 'pot-herbs' which was a few carrots and a turnip, or something like that. I never did know why it was called that. She gave me a florin, saying "Take care" as it was all she had. Well, the inevitable happened. I dropped the precious coin and, being on the hill just below our house, it rolled and went down a drain. I cried, I was so full up. Not that I should be tanned - Mum was not like that. I can't remember what she said, but how did she feel? On one occasion, a postal-order for half-a-crown came by post. We never knew where it came from, but Mum always thought it was from Aunt Susie - her mother's sister, who lived at 37 Hanover Street. Aunt Susie denied it, but she was a good sort and I think it was her. Goodness knows she could not afford it as her husband was an invalid for years - I think it was Bright's disease[2]. Anyway, that's real unsung kindness, isn't it?

I join the Army

Well, to return to the time when I left Eversheds and went to the Co-op to work. I went to London Road first and then to the Blatchington Road branch. It was nothing like the sort of trade I had been used to and I can't say that I liked it particularly. However, the year was 1914, the First World War had begun and my mates and fellow workers were leaving one by one to join the Forces. I felt alone and somehow ashamed because I was too young to join. Of course that was nothing to be ashamed of but, as always, I was perhaps over sensitive. I suppose I still am.

We lived at 74 Hanover Terrace by then and I used to walk all the way home from Blatchington Road, along Church Road to the Clock Tower, then up Queen's Road, down Trafalgar Street, and from there, home. I wish I could do it now! Anyway, one Wednesday on my half-day off, I suddenly made up my mind and went into a Recruiting

---

[2] disease of the kidneys

Office that had been opened in Church Road. I do not think I can say that it was all patriotism, but my mates had gone and I had the feeling that I was regarded as a kid, too young to do what others were doing. Mind you, I had no idea what I was letting myself in for. Inside the office there was a recruiting sergeant and an officer, as well as a medical officer. I was really scared but the sergeant asked me what I wanted, I looked so young. Then I said that I wanted to join up and he looked at me as if I should still be in my cradle. I suppose he was not far wrong! He asked my age and I boldly said "18 years". He looked at me with a smile and asked "Does your mother know that you are 18?" Then he said "All right, son, 18 it is." He took my name and passed me over to the MO who had me strip naked, and he examined and passed me. The officer then made me take the Oath of Allegiance and there I was - a soldier at 15 ¾.

A recruit was given one shilling on joining - one day's pay - known as 'taking the King's shilling'. They told me that I should get my call-up in due course. In fact it was over six months, owing to my age I expect. It's queer, as I think of it now, how impatient I was; daft little idiot! Anyway, I was finally ordered to report to Brighton Town Hall at 9 o'clock one morning.

My Mum and Dad didn't want me to join until I had to although Dad was doing a bit better by now, but they must have missed even my little contribution to the household funds, and it was thoughtless of me. I was the only one, apart from Dad, who was earning. The others (including a daughter Grace who had arrived in the meantime, the last one as it turned out), were not earning. During the War, poor old Mum had to turn out to work at six o'clock in the mornings; cleaning and scrubbing at what was then a

Canadian Hospital at the top of Elm Grove and is now the General Hospital. No, I should have thought more, although eventually I would have had to go anyway. But, wrong or not, I went then.

Chichester Barracks

Duly reporting at the Town Hall, I found around a couple of dozen others there. We were taken up the marble stairs to a large room on an upper floor. A Brigadier General (now called just 'Brigadier') came in and we were called to attention. It's a good thing we had learned that in school or we wouldn't have known how. Some soldiers! The Brigadier General gave us a talk on glorious army traditions and said that he was sure that our regiments would be proud of us after our initial training. I wonder what he really thought? We were then dismissed until 1 o'clock but, as I didn't want goodbyes all over again, I wandered about the town wondering when I should see it again. In fact it was six months later when I had my overseas leave. After we had reported back, we were marched up to Brighton Station and entrained for Chichester.

Chichester Barracks, the Royal Sussex Regiment's headquarters, seemed a dreary, forbidding place to us future 'Hopes of the Empire'. Of course once in the barracks we were under Army rule and we soon found out what that meant! Lined up on the barracks' square, we gave our names to a sergeant who then handed us over to another sergeant, a red-headed one, who was to be the bane of our lives for a time. He walked up and down the line of objects he had taken over with a look of hopeless disgust on his face. Mind you, we must have looked terrible, in all sorts of clothing; some with caps on, some with trilbys, some with no headgear at all including myself which turned out to be the best idea. One fellow even wore a bowler hat!

'Redhead' started speaking softly, then gradually rose in volume to a bull-like roar. He had never had the misfortune to see such a bunch in his life. We were a misbegotten, useless lot; we had no mothers or fathers - we were not born but spawned against a wall. He had been given the hopeless job of making soldiers out of a lot of no-good layabouts and, by God, he would do it if it killed us! He strode up and down the line, snatching off the various headgear and throwing them on the ground but when he came to the bowler hat his eyes seemed to pop out of his head. He snatched it off and stamped on it. "A soldier," he snarled, "in a bowler hat!" In a guardroom nearby was an open fire. We were ordered to march there and watch while the poor bowler hat owner cast it into the flames. His first sacrifice for his country!

The next day we paraded for uniforms - and what a 'do' that was. The quartermaster, like the NCOs of that time, was an old regular and his command of language was equal to the drill sergeant's. The tunic, trousers, shirts, underpants and puttees[3] were dished out with very little notice of size. "What size boots do you wear?" "These are too big/too small," pipes up a voice. "You'll grow to them," was the answer. Gas mask, water bottle, billy-can, entrenching tool and 'housewife' - a peculiar name I always think for a little roll of cloth containing needles and thread. However, the caps were the thing: you had one either miles

---

[3] strips of cloth wound around the legs from ankle to knee, worn to protect and support the legs

too big or too small. When we got to the barrack room, we had a sort of 'general post' and did a swap among us to get the best fit. None of us knew how to put puttees on. In the end, an old regular showed us. You see there is an art in doing it. If they are too tight they stop circulation and soon cripple you. If too loose, they fall off, and that would be a terrible crime on parade. Oh, I forgot to mention the holdall containing knife, fork, spoon, cut-throat razor, comb, lather brush and button stick, and the haversack, pack and web equipment. Proper Father Christmases we were! The rifles we had at that stage were old South African War models, rather long in the muzzle. However, we only used them for rifle drill. I and a few others were given a spell of training in map and compass reading. It was all interesting as it was a complete change from my previous life.

Training in Sherwood Forest

We were soon moved to Sittingbourne, near Maidstone in Kent, right in the middle of the fruit country. The first night was spent in the Corn Exchange at Maidstone sleeping on tables, then we were under canvas in a field near Sittingbourne. It was cold and snow came partway up the tent sides. Eventually, they moved us into billets in private houses. I was with some very nice people, the Egglestones, whose own son was already in the army in France, and I had his room. I wonder what their feelings were?

The next move was to Worksop, near Nottingham, under canvas again in the park of Thoresby Hall, a beautiful house belonging to the Earl Manvers. Up to now, we had been known as the Training Reserve, but now we were the 245th Infantry Regiment. The fellows who had been there some time had evolved a sort of initiation ceremony for newcomers, and I had to go through it. On the first evening a bunch of them got me down in the tent, pulled all my clothes off, tied me to the tent pole, and called some of the other older hands to come and see. I was very shy then and it was an ordeal. They called me a baby kid as I was so young and there were deer with fawns roaming the park. One of the favourite stunts was to put an enamel mug in someone's bed under the blanket so that when a man jumped heavily on it, it was very painful. However, we all played tricks, all meant as fun.

We spent days learning marching, physical training, bayonet fighting and, later, rifle drill and firing. There's no doubt it did me good, what with the open air and exercise. I broadened out, gained confidence and went in for boxing. By then no more liberties were taken as I could hold my own with anyone of my weight. Long route marches were a great part of training at that time and we did plenty; miles of them, singing all the way. Of course, those were the days when we never thought about things to come. Anyway, we had no idea as yet what war was, which was just as well.

The area around us was Sherwood Forest, a most lovely place noted all over the world for being the haunt of Robin Hood and his men. It seemed as though we would see Robin Hood any minute as the whole place fitted so well with the legends. There was a huge oak tree which was known as Robin Hood's larder. Whether authentic or not I don't know, but it was certainly hundreds of years old and hollow with a door cut in it. We held training in the Forest where the bracken grew taller than ourselves. It seemed such a pity that we could not be there for pleasure instead of training for war.

The Dukeries, a part of the Forest area occupied by the large old houses of the ancient nobles, was near where we trained.

The Sherwood Foresters

I should have said that we were now in the 15th Sherwood Foresters, a regiment with a fine record over hundreds of years. We were in the 3rd Battalion, a reserve unit. If a regiment was badly reduced in strength by casualties, any new men were transferred to that unit. I expect the same system is still used. The 15th had a terrible time at Ypres, as did any other unit involved there.

We eventually moved to Sheffield; a long march at night of course. As we marched into the city, dog-tired, the people came out and cheered us, showering cigarettes on us and, of all things, fish and chips! What a welcome we had. I wonder if that would happen these days, when fighting for your country is considered wrong.

We were billeted for a while in local houses, but were eventually in Hillsborough Barracks. This was, like Chichester, a real old-time barracks with no mod cons, whitewashed walls painted dark brown half way up, a very depressing jumping off place for overseas service. We had evening passes unless we were on guard duties but, at a shilling a day, we were always broke. Sheffield is a large city and, owing to the numerous steel works, every building is blackened.

One day we were paraded for active service kit and we knew what that meant. I had my first leave of one week then. I had not seen my people for nine months and naturally they were overjoyed to see me. I had not been away from home for more than a week in all my life until joining up. The bad part was of course that they knew the reason for this leave. The time went all too quickly I'm afraid.

Every summer, my second cousin Claire had been coming to stay with us. We liked each other quite a lot. She was a real beauty with golden hair, a nice figure and a lovely complexion. She was a very warm, passionate girl but I was so shy at that time that I never did more than kiss her even though she was provocative and teasing, and certainly asked for more. She wrote to me overseas but after the war she married the son of a Lord Mayor of London. I heard very little more of her. Her father-in-law was made a Baronet, a title that her husband would inherit, so I expect I was too lowly to know. She worked in a swell hairdressers in Bond Street, London, and met all the right people of course. I never had a girlfriend, apart from her. Shyness was my curse.

I hated goodbyes, and still do. Leaving that weekend was awful. Mum tried to put on a brave show but the strain for my parents must have been dreadful. I know it was for me. Honestly I think that saying goodbye to them was worse than thinking of what I might have to face in the near future. Mum and Aunt Annie came to the station with me. Mum kept her pecker up for my sake but Aunt broke down and I felt terrible. Her husband, Charlie, was already in France and it was all too much for her rather hysterical nature. The women had a lot to bear in those days. Uncle Charlie was on big siege guns in the Royal Garrison Artillery. He would have been in his forties then I think.

Well, I had to report back to Hudson Road School[4] on

---

[4] This was the headquarters for men going overseas.

my return to Sunderland. We picked up our overseas kit there and left the next day for Maidstone where I was billeted with the Egglestones again.

We entrained for Folkestone, formed up for roll call and embarked on a liner, all camouflaged with zigzag stripes. I had never been on a sea journey before, except for a ride in a paddle steamer from Brighton to Eastbourne. So this was a new experience though it would have been better if under different circumstances. It was quite a large ship, a liner taken over as a troop ship. After a roll call on deck we were issued with life jackets and told that we could go below to one of the saloons. If the ship had been sinking, how we would have floated carrying all that gear, I don't know. Of course, a soldier is committing a military crime if he loses his equipment, but I'm afraid that a lot would have been lost in an emergency like that. I know that mine would!

We cast off and made for the harbour mouth. It was evening and the ship was all blacked out with no smoking on deck. Once outside the harbour, the ship started zigzagging to make a more difficult target for torpedoes from enemy subs which were known to infest the Channel. I think that brought home the realisation of danger more than anything. It is quite a long way across the English Channel but when you are likely to be blown up and sunk in the middle of it, it seems interminable!

Most of us – there must have been thousands on board – felt happier on deck. We mostly lay about on the deck playing rummy and other card games. The sea was calm and I wasn't seasick as I feared I might be.

At Army camp, George kneeling front right

Arriving in France

In the early hours of the morning, as we entered Calais harbour, we were paraded with our kit on the decks according to whichever regiment we belonged. So, after the usual tying up and anchor dropping and with a medley of shouted orders, I set foot on the quay at Calais. My first time off British soil!

It's a queer thing, but French places have a look, which I had imagined they would have. One could never forget and think that it was an English place. Yet there were the quays, the cranes, the bollards and all the impedimenta, the same as Folkestone. There definitely is something about the Continent.

After another roll call, we were marched through some streets to what looked like a large open space, all dry sand, there seemed to be miles of it, somewhere behind the harbour. We took over a large camp where the tents had been vacated by some poor baskets who had moved on to warmer climes. What a mixed lot there were from various units, including Highlanders who sat on the sand moaning because, believe it or not, they did not wear anything under the kilt and all their lower parts were smothered in sand!

While we were there, a fellow scraped about in the sand in his tent and found an old Mills grenade buried underneath. The pin must have rusted away and he blew himself, an officer and four other men to pieces. Killed without even seeing the fighting. Queer how fate works things out for some of us.

When we moved, it was by train in cattle trucks with no windows. We crept along. If nature called, you had time to jump down, answer the call, and run and catch up.

Anyway, who wanted to hurry to where we were going?

The railroad only operated up to a certain point as it could not go near the area of hostilities. Our stop was a small town, which turned out to be Poperinge, in Belgium, not far from Ypres. By now we certainly knew what war looked like, at least from a distance. In the direction where Ypres lay, the whole sky was a blaze of red and yellow. The gunfire was incessant and the earth shook with the force of explosions. That was my first sight of war and Ypres.

We alighted and army-like had to form up in the market square which was surrounded by houses of obvious Flemish design, not a lot damaged up until then. The town suffered mostly from what was called 'hate strafings': sudden bursts of shelling lasting about ten minutes. Of course the Jerries knew that the town was a jumping-off point for troops for Ypres so naturally they were going to make it as uncomfortable as possible. Also, if a few of us were killed, well all the fewer to fight against them. On this occasion it was an 'off' spell so for the short time we were there we were left alone.

In the square opposite the station one of the houses had been made into a sort of rest centre, although what time a front line soldier had to rest I never discovered. Anyway, the idea was good and they gave us a nice cup of tea and a bit of food if we felt like it. It was founded by the brother and a friend of an officer who had been killed in 1915 and was called Talbot House in his memory, later shortened to the signallers' abbreviation of TocH. There was nothing churchy about it, just a sort of last outpost before the fray[5].

---

[5] After the War, some of the British men who had benefited from Talbot House set up a charity organisation called 'TocH' to create opportunities and help people from all walks of life. TocH continues to operate today.

Talbot House: a soldier's sketch Courtesy of www.greatwar.co.uk

To Ypres and real war

At dusk, we set off on the last leg of the journey to the Ypres sector and real war. Surely nothing could be more miserable or depressing than that journey up to the line. There was no real front line, trenches could not be dug in mud. The Belgians had broken their canal banks to hold up the German advance but of course it worked both ways. The mud was so deep that if a man slipped off the 18 inch wide duckboards, which had been mostly blown away by shellfire anyway, he would sink as if in quicksand and was often lost for good. A white tape had originally been put down as a guide to our sector, but that soon disappeared into the mud and it was too easy to get lost if one slipped as the single column must keep moving.

I slipped and managed to struggle out but by then the column of men had gone and in the dark I seemed to be alone. Was I scared? I certainly was. Of course I must not shout or make any noise and I seemed to be hours wandering and slipping. All I dared was a hoarse whisper, "Any Sherwoods here?" After what seemed an age, a voice said quietly, "Shut up you silly bastard." I went towards the voice and found that it was the Battalion HQ of one of the Highland regiments in a cellar, which was all that was left of a farmhouse. I had to stay with them until a battalion runner was going up to the line. He took me to where my lot were. Of course they thought I had gone in the mud or deserted! However, I eventually joined my own mob in the front line.

There was no real line as in the Somme sector, owing to the flooding from the broken canal banks. We were crouched in cellars of buildings of which the upper parts had been almost or totally destroyed. The ruins of the larger buildings, such as the Cloth Hall, a very ancient and beautiful place, stuck up like a lot of broken teeth. The whole awful scene was constantly lit by the exploding of shells and the noise combined with the vibration was terrible. It seemed to my young mind what hell would be like.

During the whole of the war, Ypres and its remains changed hands over and over again. In the process, thousands of men of both sides lost their lives. My future father-in-law, who was in the Seaforth Highlanders, was missing in that campaign and never heard of again. Mostly, men whose bodies were never found were said to have 'had a shell to themselves'. In other words, blown to pieces. What waste.

As it happened, 25 years after that war began, there was another one. Although not so many fighting men were killed, thousands of civilians were when unprotected towns were bombed. Of course war is wrong and wasteful, but what if the Germans had been allowed to take over the world in 1914? It is true that there would have been no Hitler because they would already have had Europe, but obviously it would not have stopped there. Look at the world today. Every country wants the whole or a piece of their neighbours' territory. I am afraid there will always be wars. Too many of all races want power over others. There have been wars ever since before Christianity and I cannot see them stopping. Greed for power is the main cause, but however patriotic, courageous and willing to fight for his native land a man may be, he never seems to benefit.

Of the battles of the First War in Europe, I think that men like myself, who have served on both European fronts, would agree that Ypres was the worst. Apart from the danger to our lives, the conditions we fought in were foul beyond imagination.

My first time up the line lasted two weeks. Then, those who lived to do so, struggled out under fire to a spot a mile or two behind the line for a so-called rest. This was supposed to be a week during which we scraped some of the mud off us, deloused ourselves as much as possible and got ready to go through it all again. Often though, if the troops who took over from us had a bad time with the loss of many men, back into the line we had to go even if we had only been out for a day. Of course it couldn't be helped but it was a dreadful strain.

Rations were a problem too. Often the ration wagons, which were mostly horse-drawn at that time, were wiped out on the journey. The only way we would know was when no food turned up. It was only horseflesh cut into squares and put in sandbags and one loaf between three men, but it just kept us alive. If it was not there for a day or two, bad as it was, you missed it. The meat used to be covered in hairs from the sandbags and they had to be scraped off before it could be eaten. It shows what you will eat if half starved. Sometimes it would be a 12 oz tin of bully beef between three. As a treat, a tin of lemon marmalade came up. Always lemon, I don't know why. Since then I have never liked lemon marmalade.

Our life was a series of backwards and forwards for months. Capture a bit of ruin, lose it, get it again. Sheer monotony of danger, mud and nerve strain. After a month or two of this, during which we had lost a great number of troops, we were moved to various places in the sector, all equally beastly. Where the Menin Gate memorial now stands was a real suicide spot. Death came from snipers in ruined buildings, whizzbangs, minenwerfers[6] and long distance shelling. Occasionally a plane would fly almost on top of us; the pilot would lean over holding a machine gun in his hand, while still piloting the plane, and give us a burst of fire practically point blank. They were quite marvellous in their way but we hadn't a hope. We would fire our rifles at them they were so close, but with little

---

[6] minenwerfer – a trench mortar

35

effect. There were 'dog fights' above us between our little planes and theirs. With the craft they had in those days, both sides were heroes! Then there were the observation balloons, with a poor devil suspended in a basket under them. Both sides would fire at the gasbags which burst into flames. Not a hope for the poor bloke in the basket.

Diphtheria

On one occasion we were out on a 'rest' for a few days – the first for three weeks. We stayed in a small collection of Nissen huts set in terrible mud and filth and with the nasty smell of slimy mud and unburied bodies which were always turning up. There were pools of slimy water all around. With rations being held up, some of us boiled this water in our billycans to make tea of a sort. Our tea and sugar ration used to come up mixed together so you just put it in your canteen with water on top and boiled it up on one of those methylated burners, like large tins of Vaseline, if you had one.

What happened was really inevitable looking back now. Our army was hard pressed on a number of fronts. Thousands were being killed and wounded, more and more men were needed. There was neither the time nor the place for troops to rest, clean up or re-equip. Two or three of my company developed sore throats and, in the usual way with hard pressed MOs, little notice was taken of it. Medicine and duty, they said, which interpreted meant…nothing. However, myself and two others found difficulty in swallowing, so the MO must have got the wind up and sent swabs down to base.

A couple of days later we were actually being made to do physical jerks on the slimy ground, when a flustered

MO dashed out. Our company Sergeant Major bawled out three names: mine, my mate Jack Warner's and another, named Henshall. Talk about wind up! We had to get our kit together double quick. An ambulance arrived from base. We were loaded on, and off. Diphtheria - no wonder the panic. The whole army could have gone down with it. What a windfall for the enemy if that had happened!

We went right down to the coast of France. It turned out to be Boulogne. We were examined there, then taken to a small seaside resort nearby called Wimereux, a summer spot for wealthy tourists in peacetime. There was a small hospital there but they had no room for isolation cases so we three were each put in a delightful bathing chalet on the beach. If we had been well, it would have been lovely! I think they were scared to death of us coming into contact with any other troops. Who can blame them? The whole army could have been *hors de combat* in a short while if it had spread.

Well, we were only kept at Wimereux for a few days but, if we had been in good health, I would have liked to stay for months. After the battlefields, to lie in that little chalet and hear the sea washing to and fro on the sandy shore was like heaven. Even the gunfire was very distant.

Return to England

At St Denis we were put aboard a hospital ship in a day or two and started our zigzag run back across the Channel to Folkestone. Being confined to bed and of course below decks all the time, I felt more afraid of a torpedo attack than during my previous crossing. So helpless. In fact we would not have had much hope.

It was dark when we arrived. The cliffs of England

look very different under those conditions. No lights showing a welcome and hardly a sound, almost unbelievably quiet. Folkestone, Blighty, again!

We were a mixed bag on the ship, wounded and seriously sick. The three diptheria cases had of course been kept apart on the boat and when we landed we were loaded onto a hospital train going north. Our destination turned out to be Stockport, Cheshire, not far from Manchester. The Isolation Hospital was part of what had been the Infirmary and was now the General Hospital. Being in a Midland regiment, I was always put up north so never once were my people able to afford to come and see me, ill or wounded. It worried them and was disappointing for me.

We three were put in observation wards, glass on three sides. No one but the doctors and nurses were allowed near us. I had a silver tube down my throat which was taken out and cleaned frequently. Life was a series of throat swabbings, partial choking and bad heads. I must have been too ill to know much. Weeks went by which I do not even remember. I was told afterwards that it had been touch and go for myself and the others.

When we were improving, we found out how good everyone at the hospital had been to us. Literally fighting for our lives! Henshall said it was only because so many were being killed and they needed us back over there, but I don't think that was all.

For convalescence we were sent to a VAD hospital in a house belonging to the Earl of Ingestre, near Manchester, where they were very good to us. People sent their cars to take us to their big houses for tea and to theatres. The churches organised entertainments for us and obviously proud to do it.

It is a fact that, in those days, a soldier fighting for his country was worthy of the best; when he was here to receive it. Since that time, things have altered greatly. It seems to be a crime to be proud of one's country. What a pity it is.

Overseas service again

When considered fit, we Sherwoods were sent to our depot at Hudson Road Schools in Sunderland to re-equip for overseas service again. While there we were attached to the 3rd Sherwoods, the home-based supply battalion. Naturally in that anxious period of the war, we were not kept there long. Within a week or two, we were once more equipped on a train to the south, on a ship at Folkestone and off to that haven of peace: France.

After the usual zigzag journey we landed this time at Le Havre. There were the usual roll calls and parades. Then we were, at least I was, sent to join the 1/8th Battalion Sherwoods. They had lost a great number of men in the battles of the Somme so I and some others, unknown to me, were transferred to fill the gaps.

According to some who had served there, the Somme sector was certainly no picnic, but I thought it could not possibly be as bad as the Ypres area. I soon found out that if any battleground can be better than another as regards the state of the ground and the absence of that awful mud, this was better. For one thing, we had trenches as a bit of protection whereas trenches could certainly not be dug in the quagmire of Ypres.

Of course, as I have said, we always had to march so far on the way to the front line. There were no transports for troops so, when we were a couple or so miles from it, we went the rest of the way in single file. Up to that point, we were singing all the old songs which were favourites at that time: *Tipperary*, *There's a long long trail a-winding*, *Keep the home fires burning*, *I wanna go home*, *Mam'sel from Armentiers*, *If you want the Sergeant Major we know where he is*, and a number of very vulgar versions of those and others.

The country was still undamaged for miles at that time. It was agricultural land with here and there a lovely little village in the traditional French style. A little church, a farm, a blacksmith's, an *estaminet* or inn, and sometimes a lovely chateau or castle belonging to the owner of the surrounding property. It was winter when I first saw the Somme district. It was attractive then but in the summer, in peacetime, it must have been beautiful.

As we approached the fighting area though, there were signs of how the land and the people had suffered. Some places were not yet damaged but the occupants had fled as the war got closer. If we halted for a few minutes we sometimes looked inside some of the houses in a deserted town or village. It is a most peculiar experience to be in an absolutely deserted town especially if it is so far undamaged. In particular I remember Bethune, quite a large town. We entered it in daylight, went single file down silent streets and, although one could hear the guns much louder now, the silence in the town itself seemed ghostly. It impressed me more I think because it was undamaged, like a place in *The Sleeping Beauty*. You expected someone to come out of one of the houses any minute. Out on the road here and there were piles of furniture and precious belongings which the owners had hoped to take with them but found that there was no room on their carts.

We went inside some houses and most were still fully furnished. In one or two cases, a partly consumed meal was still on the table. It reminded me of the story of the *Marie Celeste*, as though there must be people there. Poor devils, leaving their homes and treasured possessions at a moment's notice, knowing that they would never see them again and that their house and home would almost certainly be blown to pieces as the battle moved back and forth over the town.

I was still only a boy really and it affected me more at the time than the danger to come. I suppose I was a sentimental fool. I still am. The fact that I am putting my thoughts on paper like this proves once more that I am what is sneered at these days: a nostalgic, sentimental old fool! However, I am as I am and now too old to change.

Some of the country we went through on our way to the line was beautiful farmland. Later, in the summer, our trenches were dug through ripening corn fields, never to be harvested. What a pity it was. Poor France and Belgium, doomed to another dose of it 20 odd years' later.

The Somme

Our battalion's first trenches on the Somme were cut right through the ruins of a village. In fact our platoon's part was dug through a churchyard, continuing through the cellar of what I understood was the priest's house.

Having completed a machine gun and Lewis gun course at Manston after my sick leave, I was not now a rifleman, but a member of a four man machine gun section under a corporal.

Our part of the trench was at intervals strafed by quick firing guns. The report of the gun and the explosion of the shells was so close together that they were known as 'whizzbangs'. Everything the Germans did was methodical. The spells of shelling came at such regular intervals that you could set your watch by them. Anyway, all one could do was crouch down under what was dignified by the name of dugout, which was usually an odd scrap of corrugated iron scrounged from somewhere with a few sandbags on top, laid over a hole laboriously cut out of the back of the trench. Of course, it only provided protection against flying pieces of shell casing or shrapnel. A direct hit and we would have had it. I suppose we were like ostriches, buried our heads in the sand and hoped for the best!

Except for the periodic shelling, we were in what could be called a quiet sector. We even had our field kitchen concealed behind a few trees which had so far survived, with our company cook making the everlasting bully beef stew.

I wandered into what was left of the house one day. The furniture was still there, although some of the building had been reduced to rubble. There were beds upstairs with the big box mattresses which the French people seemed so fond of sleeping on. The owners' little ornaments and personal treasures were all there, but they certainly never saw them again. Jerry sent over a number of big ones a week or two after we took over; killed four of our chaps, including our cook, and blew the house to blazes. All we found of our cook was his boots, helmet and identity discs. The field kitchen was just scrap iron.

We already had to co-exist with bones and broken coffins from the churchyard. In some places skeletons stuck out of the sides of our trench, but we got used to it.

Rats too were things we got used to. They fed on unburied corpses and grew as big as large kittens. Then of course there were the lice which got into every seam in a man's clothes, bred like the devil, and nearly drove us crazy! We were not able to wash ourselves or our clothes and that encouraged them. When you have been used to being clean, it is just another form of torture. However, we were all in the same boat, officers too.

Merry Hell

Inevitably we were soon moved to a more 'lively' spot where, although we didn't know it, the brass hats were preparing for an offensive. So another lot took over our little spot and off we went. The piece of line we took over, so our outgoing predecessors told us with unconcealed relish, was called 'merry hell'. No peace, day or night. They had raids by small groups of Jerries every night and intermittent shelling all day and had been waiting three weeks to be relieved. As they left, they kindly wished us the best of luck and got out as quickly as they could.

It was a hot shop, there's no doubt about that. The other lot hadn't had any rations for three days because the ration chaps were wiped out on the way up. This was quite a common occurrence and sometimes the line troops were practically starving. When relieving, the ingoing troops would file silently into the trench and the outgoing would squeeze past them the other way. Of course silence was important, as when the enemy knew, and he always did seem to know, he would play hell, trying to wipe out as many as possible. I am not blaming Jerry, both sides did it. After all, it was a part of self-preservation.

Our section corporal was named Lambert. He wasn't

a bad NCO, but a poor blighter with any chevrons at all automatically becomes a bastard according to the men under him, especially if he's keen on discipline. There's nothing in it really, just a habit, when anyone holds rank of even a minor degree.

The usual thing on taking over a trench was a search for the best dugouts, such as they were. The NCOs naturally used their rank to have first choice and the stronger men had the next, all in the natural scheme of things. It was the habit of our platoon sergeant and corporals to try for a dugout together. We three remaining members of the gun section had just found a place for ourselves and dumped ourselves in it, when our Corporal Lambert came along saying that he, another corporal and a lance corporal had already staked their claim there. Of course we objected and there was much swearing. We gave in, found another and would soon have forgotten all about it, but we had hardly found a likely spot when there was a scream of whizzbangs. We all ducked. One scored a direct hit on our trench, too near for comfort.

We crawled along the trench. It was the dugout we would have had and Lambert, who was the sole occupant at the time, was lying half-buried in the shell hole. One leg was blown off as cleanly as if cut with a knife. His face looked unmarked but he was as dead as a doornail from the blast. And that is how I became a corporal in a Lewis and machine gun section.

From then on I had no rifle but carried a revolver which, although I was a first class shot with a rifle, I found the very devil to master. Eventually I just about got by.

I should mention that our CO, a colonel whose name I cannot call to mind, was very keen on physical fitness and one of his ideas was, no doubt rightly, that cigarette smoking was bad for stamina. So when we were on the march out of the line, no smoking was allowed - except with a pipe. We were in Albert at the time so we all descended on the shops of the town and must have bought all the pipes in the place. Of course in the line there were mostly only issue fags to be had, very little pipe tobacco, so we had to smoke those or nothing. However, since that time, now over 50 years ago, I have always smoked a pipe. In that period you could get tobacco as cheap as fourpence an ounce and fags at ten for tuppence. Those were the days!

A succession of wars has led to rise after rise in prices of everything and they will certainly never go down to that level again.

Patrolling No Man's Land

It was the custom to periodically send out patrols at night into No Man's Land with the objective of finding out any little thing about the enemy: disposition of troops, strong points and, if possible, capture a prisoner, who was doing the same thing. Usually a patrol consisted of three men and one officer. Wire cutters were taken to cut a small gap in our barbed wire through which we crawled. I must confess that of all the unpleasant duties that came our way, this was the most hated.

Absolute silence was necessary. This was no easy achievement when, in the dark, a man did not know what debris of a battlefield he was crawling over. Often bodies of men from both sides would lie for weeks in No Man's Land and rot. I remember crawling on all fours on one patrol and putting my hand right on the rotted face of some poor devil who was most likely killed on such a caper as we were on at that moment. British or German I didn't know, but it had been a man like us. Used as we all became to death, horrible disgusting death, planting your hand in a decomposing face would turn anyone's stomach. Mercifully there was seldom time to dwell on it.

The idea was to get very close to the enemy trench and listen. Usually the officer knew at least a little of the German language and we would lie silent, hardly daring to breathe. A few bits of conversation between the German troops might give information as to their regiment and intentions. Whether anything useful was ever picked up I never knew, but if they were anything like our lot, they never knew what was going to happen until an hour or so before it came off, for security reasons. We could hear the rattle of the German limbers[7] at the rear of their line bringing up supplies, the clinking of equipment and an occasional laugh.

One of the dangers to both sides' patrols were the Verey lights. They were a type of rocket fired from a Verey pistol which would reach a great height and then float down to give a brilliant white light over miles of the battle area. This threw everything in No Man's Land into an appearance of bright moonlight. If a movement was seen, all machine gun posts opened up on the unfortunate patrol. Once spotted you had very little hope of getting back to your line. Occasionally we would get a prisoner and take him back to our line for interrogation or they would get one of ours, but not often.

During the following months we captured the enemy lines, held them for a while, lost them, gained them. That

[7] limbers - the forward part of a gun carriage to which the horses are attached, and carrying ammunition

also happened in reverse of course. Trench warfare was like that, until a really big offensive came off. In that case, either side might advance for miles, dig into the captured line and fight like hell to hang on through heavy shelling from the other side who were trying to drive you out.

All this meant much loss of life and increasing difficulty in getting supplies and rations to us. If an army is advancing very fast, it is almost impossible for munitions and rations to keep up. The enemy naturally is shelling behind your advancing troops to hold up reserves who would be coming to strengthen your depleted forces. In other words, it is not all honey when holding a captured position. There is no relaxing. You have to be on the alert all the time. Usually a sentry was placed at three yard intervals along the captured line, now being used in reverse: what had been the back of the German trench was now the front of ours.

I remember being on guard in such a situation where I was right beside a German machine gun complete with all its team; all dead but in such a life-like position that one expected them to move at any minute. It was a moonlit night with a lull in the gunfire and, although I had become used to death, it gave me the creeps.

We had been moderately successful lately and had made many advances in our sector, which meant casualties. A great number of my battalion had been killed or wounded and so had left us. We were overdue for relief, things were hotting up and we could sense that a large-scale attack by our division was coming. Officially we never knew until the night before that a 'do' was coming, but there was a sort of jungle telegraph which operated from goodness knows where.

St Omer and a short reprieve

The weather now was glorious. It was spring and to our surprise we were moved back, partly on foot as usual, then in cattle trucks, to St Omer. It was a lovely old town which, though badly damaged in the early days of the war, was a wonderful sight for us after months of seeing little but ruins. I remember the old market square where stalls were still open, selling things we had not seen for ages. We were set free to wander around the stalls and, as we had just had our first pay for months, about 20 francs (a franc was worth about tenpence then), we went on a spree. At a stall, a pal and I bought some butter and a French loaf which was about three-quarters of a yard long. Then we went to an *estaminet* and bought some *vin blanc* and made pigs of ourselves.

We were billeted in all sorts of places. My company was in an old tannery. There were great tanks in the floor in which leather was soaked. The smell was unpleasant, but who cared? It had smelled worse where we came from!

We spent about three days there, mostly used in refitting and replacing ruined uniforms. It seems strange to anyone outside the Forces that even if a regiment is out of the front line for only a day or two, boots and equipment, including buttons, have to be cleaned up. The reason was good, although we didn't see it at the time. Knowing what would be in front of us and after all the danger and tension of the past months, suddenly being idle would have been very bad for morale. Oh yes, I can see that after all these years, but few of us did at the time.

I could relate thousands of incidents that occurred in the weeks and months which followed. The courage of my mates, the awful deaths of some of them and the total obliteration of others because, make no mistake, although new high explosives have been invented in recent years, a man or even a whole company could be wiped out with those big shells. Not a shred of any man would be left. I know this to be true, having seen it with my own frightened eyes when I was a boy of 17 in years, but certainly a man in experience.

Taking Thiepval

My battalion rejoined our division, the 46th North Midland, at Pozieres. They had been attacking every day since the offensive began in July. Casualties had been enormous, but they had advanced a great distance. It really looked as though things were going the way of the Allies at last. The present offensive was designed to take the pressure off the French who had been having a bad time on their front. They took a terrible pounding for weeks.

The 46th Division's first objective after our 1/8th Sherwoods rejoined them was Thiepval, or what was left of it. We had taken over trenches that were cut through Thiepval wood which had been changing hands often during the campaign, but surprisingly there were still a few sizeable stumps of trees left. One might think that it would be an advantage to have trenches in a wood for concealment. The reverse is true though as the enemy has a fine target for his big guns. Did he shell those woods? He pounded them night and day. Trees were blown, root and all, into the air and a lot of troops with them. We hated fighting from woods but even worse in my opinion is hand-to-hand fighting in a wood. I had one or two doses of that and I did not like it.

Being Corporal in charge of a Lewis gun section, I and my merry men were, as usual with machine gun teams, positioned slightly in front of what was left of our trench, in a shellhole with a rough parapet of sandbags. It's a strange thing but the Commanders in Chief did not think that machine guns were of any use! They should have had to face the German ones as we had to.

Unfortunately nearly all of the High Command were cavalry men and knew little about that type of war. I am sure that thousands of men, poor devils of infantry chaps like us, were wiped out owing to the out-of-date cavalry ideas. When they finally gave in we were only allowed four guns per company. With a little bit of cover one machine gun can defend a large area, traversing in a wide sweep with deadly precision. We had experienced it from their guns so we knew what could be done with ours. The extreme dislike of being opposite the wrong end of a machine gun naturally made each of the opposing forces try to wipe them out as quickly as possible. So not only were we the object of special strafing, but that in turn made our own chaps give us as wide a berth as they could. A lonely but very essential lot, we gunners.

We went over the top at dawn as usual to try to take Thiepval itself. The noise during a big attack is quite unbelievable unless one has experienced it. All along the miles of front our guns opened up: the huge siege guns miles behind us, and the lighter artillery nearer to our reserve line. Our people were using the recently invented 'creeping barrage'. I will explain this as well as an infantry man can. A short time before the troops went over, the big guns would pound the enemy's reserve lines in order to stop troops and supplies moving up. Just before the attack proper began, the guns would cease and then, as the troops went over the parapet, the whole barrage of guns opened up again, this time a short distance in front of our men. The line of exploding shells would then move forward at a comparatively safe distance from the advancing men and the troops moved slowly behind the barrage as it crept forward. The idea was to provide a screen of fire to cover our advance and to prevent a counter attack by the Germans. It usually worked too, as long as no big gun slipped up in their range finding and some of the troops did not advance too quickly. But the noise! It was a marvellous thing that our eardrums still worked afterwards. It's about the nearest thing to an inferno I can think of. Unfortunately some men were bound to be killed by shell splinters from our own barrage, but not so many as would have been killed by the Germans if they were not busy taking cover.

On this occasion we got to the German front line to find that the trench was occupied by a few very live troops. They had obviously had lots of casualties from the barrage which was now some way away pounding the ruins behind Jerry's lines. There was some hand-to-hand fighting, not pleasant in the confined space of a trench. Some were killed in their trench, some ran back, and we took a few prisoners who were sent back under escort to our rear.

Well, we had got their trench, but our orders were to keep moving after them to their second and third lines. Our following troops took over as we moved on. So over the top we went once more. The barrage had now stopped and the enemy had retreated. In fact apart from their dead and ours, there were few men in sight. Of course based on previous experience we knew what had happened. The ruins of Thiepval lay in front and they would be waiting for us under cover of what was left of the buildings - a very pleasant outlook!

As we neared the town, machine guns opened up and this was joined by rifle fire from the buildings. One of my mates went down near me, shot through the head. Contrary to stories and motion pictures, you are not expected or allowed to stop with your dying comrade. For one thing, there is not time in the type of war fought these days.

A few yards in front of the town a machine gun was keeping up a murderous fire and holding us up as well as causing enormous casualties. The CO of our company, a captain, was hit in the belly. Of all the horrible deaths, that is terrible to suffer and to see. He stood bolt upright and his screams, even in the surrounding din, were awful to hear. Death from wounds in the abdomen are not only the most painful way of dying, but the most drawn out.

That gun was holding up the advance along that sector and something had to be done about it. Our platoon officer, named Lieutenant Shackleton if I remember rightly, asked me and my team to go forward, clean them out and establish our gun there. Of course none of us wanted that job, but at the rate things were going, if *it* was not stopped then *we* would be - permanently.

We crawled forward, my number two carrying our gun, my number three the ammunition, me with my trusty revolver hoping I was a good enough shot with it to kill before I was killed. They were located in a deep shellhole, so we could not see them. The gun was obviously poking out of a crevice. On the spur of the moment I decided to try bombing them before attempting to get inside the hole. We didn't even know how many were holed up in there.

At a signal from me, all four of us lobbed in Mills

grenades from about six yards away, then lay flat. The resulting explosion was terrific, accompanied by screams and pieces of debris. After a wait to let things settle, we clambered over the edge of the crater. In peacetime the sight would have turned my stomach, but in the stress of war there is no time to feel any emotion. It's the same when one of your mates is killed beside you, there is a sort of fatalism. No one I knew was of a cruel nature. It's a case of self preservation - them or you. Both sides knew it and we all accepted the fact.

Inside the crater was a shambles. There must have been about eight men there before we bombed them. All but two were dead. One of the two was an officer wearing the ribbon of the Iron Cross, as all German officers seemed to. I think the other man was a private soldier. Both had their hands above their heads when we clambered into the crater. Lieutenant Shackleton and I, as officer and NCO, went forward to take from the German officer the revolver which he held out towards us.

It's a funny thing, but in circumstances like that we had no fear of treachery, taking it for granted that, as they were surrendering with hands up, they would keep to the now seemingly out-of-date war code of honour. But no, I went toward the private to see if he was armed and Shackleton went to the officer. Immediately my man whipped a grenade from his belt and prepared to pull out the pin. I acted on impulse and tried to grab it. He gave me a violent push. I fell over a number of bodies and rolled to the edge of the crater. In the meantime, Lieutenant Shackleton struggled with his German opposite number who had tried to shoot him. Shackleton shot him in the head. The private threw the grenade to his right. My officer and I dived to the ground. The explosion seemed to lift me up and dump me outside the hole. Shackleton landed near me. We were both stunned but lucky beyond words. I had a bomb splinter in my thigh and Shackleton had a leg injured, but by all rules we should have been well and truly dead.

Anyway, our troops could now move forward to attempt the capture of the town. Good luck to them. We two men struggled back to the nearest dressing station.

Awarded the Military Medal

I had a piece of grenade casing taken out of my abdomen and a piece out of my thigh, but that was a light injury compared with what would have happened if I had not been blown clear by the blast. I should certainly have been, like the Germans and two of my chaps, blown to pieces.

As regards courage, I did not feel brave, cool or fearless. As I have said, it's a matter of self-preservation. If you don't kill them, they will kill you. It's as simple as that. If we tell the truth, every one of us was afraid all through the war but in the tension under which we existed, there was never time to show it. I never believe anyone, in whatever circumstances, who states that they are never afraid.

I spent a month in hospital at Etaples being patched up. While I was in hospital I heard that Lieutenant Shackleton was given the Military Cross. I and the only remaining member of my team were awarded the Military Medal[8]. But to be alive after that was reward enough. I

---

[8] The Military Medal was instituted by King George V on 25th March 1916, "as a medal to be awarded to non-commissioned officers and men for individual or associated acts of bravery on the recommendation of a Commander-in-Chief in the Field." (British Gallantry Awards, PE Abbott, JMA Tamplin, publ. Guinness Superlatives Ltd in conjunction with BA Seaby Ltd, 1971.)

never saw my officer again.

I was back with my battalion in a month, in the thick of it. Such is life, luck and death in war. The loss of men was terrible. We were patched up if possible and sent into the fray again. It was lovely weather, late summer, corn ripe in the fields and blue skies overhead. But the struggle continued and our troops were pushing on.

All the lives: All the hardship

The objective at the time I rejoined was a German trench, thought to be part of the Hindenburg Line of reputedly impregnable trenches that stretched for miles. Behind this, the Germans had been well dug in and fairly safe all through the war. I don't think they ever expected to be disturbed as there were so many well-fortified lines, also said to be impregnable, to be broken first. However, our troops had advanced at such a pace that we were threatening even parts of that line which they thought we would never reach. A well kept secret was the first occasion of our going over the top with tanks and I am sure that, for once, the Germans were taken by surprise. We went over in the usual open formation just behind them. They looked wonderful as they lumbered across No Man's Land ahead of us, into shell craters and out the other side with the greatest of ease. When they reached the enemy trench they went right through the wire, over the trench, and on to the next line, machine guns firing all the time. The Germans really were scared, and so should we have been! A totally new and unexpected monster coming right over every obstacle, and they could not stop it. We, following, had no trouble at all in driving them out of their trenches and beyond. We advanced miles that day.

The great fault with the tanks, once the surprise element was over, was their comparative slowness and size. Once the Germans realised this and got their range, they scored direct hits on a lot of them. If they were not blown to pieces, they were disabled and were then sitting targets. The occupants were literally roasted alive as their vehicle was set on fire. Of course our Command soon realised this and in time a smaller, faster one was made, known as the whippet tank. These were more successful; but there is no doubt in my mind that once the initial surprise was over their effectiveness diminished. Naturally, the Germans soon had fast tanks themselves. Our first ones were a fine idea, but were not fast enough in manoeuvring.

As we pushed further into country which the Germans had held since the early days of the war, we were amazed at the comfort of their reserve positions. Very deep tunnels with high roofed rooms had been carved out of the soil. In the officers' quarters there were two-tier bunks with wire netting bottoms, and even a straw-filled mattress. We hadn't seen such luxury for ages. Stairs led down to most of them. I found German magazines with cartoons of our King and High Command, not complimentary either, and pin-up pictures of naked girls too. No, there's not much difference in men, whatever the nation.

Through that autumn of 1917 the Allied Forces ploughed on. Thousands of prisoners were taken. In fact, so many were captured and sent back behind our lines that it was impossible for the line troops to provide escorts for them. I suppose they did get there - we were too busy at the time to know. On one occasion, our platoon sergeant, a good fellow, a Mansfield man named Gender, was forming up a hundred or two of them to be taken back, when shells from the Germans' own guns scored a direct hit on them. It killed nearly all of them and, unfortunately, the sergeant as well. We had naturally lain down flat when the salvo started and we didn't know about Sergeant Gender until the Company Commander pointed out his body to me, saying "There's your Sergeant". He had been blown against a bank and the blast had split his abdomen from neck to thighs, as though cut with a knife. All his intestines were outside and flies were already on them. Knowing him so well, it affected me more than anything I had seen before. The events culminating in his death took place on 10th September 1917, my birthday. What a celebration. I can hear him now, after all these years, calling our platoon together: "Fall in cat" - his version of 'four' in French, for Number Four Platoon.

Well, no purpose is served by going over everything that happened in the winter months that followed. It was a bitter winter and nothing much was doing. We just huddled up and tried to keep warm. The winter battlefield looked, if possible, worse than the summer. Broken towns and villages, torn-up churchyards. The large French calvaries dotted here and there along the roadside were strangely still standing, although some were leaning over, even after most other things had gone. The little grottoes which were placed to shelter images of the Holy Mother often survived. Our Christmas surroundings!

The spring of 1918, after a wet start, was an improvement. We were wet instead of frozen.

In March 1918, the disillusionment came. The Germans launched a terrific offensive, driving everything before them. In a matter of weeks we had lost all, and more, of the gains we had struggled to make. It was the nearest to panic that I had seen during my overseas service. We were ordered to retreat to first one position, then back to another. Artillery, mostly at that time horse-drawn, tore right through our retreating troops, not seeming to know where they were going, the horses looking wild with fear. We were in danger of being killed by them as we crouched close to the edge of a road.

Regiments were broken up into small groups who had lost their way. Some of them joined us and we became a bedraggled, mixed group. Most of our equipment had been lost, including rations, and most of us hadn't even a razor. A retreat is very demoralizing and we were all at a very low ebb. Our armies were driven almost back to the coast and Jerry nearly made it to Paris. Conditions were the same, if not worse, than in the autumn of 1914, before I went to France, when the enemy nearly reached Paris and the Allies were forced into headlong retreat. So there we were, all the lives, all the hardship, and all to do again!

Relics of war

The line was held with a thin sprinkling of troops, many miles back from our old front line of years before. We came across relics of the early days from 1914/15. Once we found an old trench and a dugout which had collapsed during shelling in those early days of war. Inside was still a clear space, only the entrance had been blocked preventing the occupants from getting out, or even breathing for long. There were three men in there sitting on the floor in quite natural positions, with rifles beside them. The rifles were of the 1914/15 period, before the Lee Enfield 303s were issued, and they had no steel helmets, which again were not issued until a later date, but they did have the first gas protection masks, just a piece of flannel to tie over the mouth. Our first ones were flannel bags which went right over our heads, with a tube which you put into your mouth. You then breathed in through your nose and out through the mouthpiece. The whole thing was soaked in a solution supposed to minimise the effect of poison gas. Most uncomfortable things.

The bodies we found had mummified. The skin had yellowed and tightened over the bones. There was no smell. The place must have been airtight for three years, preserving the bodies and uniforms. It was a strange sight.

It was mid-summer when the Allied Forces were sufficiently ready, re-equipped and reinforced to take the offensive. It simply had to be successful or we would be driven into the sea. The offensive opened with a bang: we now had more Lewis guns and machine guns, faster tanks and more motor transport. We had lost a lot of equipment in the March retreat which we could ill afford to lose. Now there was a hard fight over the same torn battlefield we had previously gained and which had cost thousands of lives.

My division was still to serve on the Somme front and at first we were in reserve, being reinforced by young troops from England and overseas troops. Once things got going there was no rest. We attacked night and day, twice a day. We really did make headway. By the beginning of August we had recaptured a lot of lost territory. The Americans had arrived in late 1917 but, owing to reorganisation at base and then the catastrophe of March 1918, their arrival had no noticeable effect, which was not their fault.

As an old campaigner looking back, I think that, apart

from anything the Americans were to actually do in that last year of war, the news that fresh troops had arrived, however inexperienced, had a great effect on the German morale. After all, like us, they had experienced four years of hard fighting, wretched conditions, and on top of that the disappointment after their great push of March. Whatever the cause, the spirit of our opponents was not the same, and I do not blame them. There is little doubt in my mind that, win or lose, there is a psychology within an army. For instance, when we were making headway before March, despite all the filth, death and danger, we managed to keep in good spirits with the usual grim jokes about everything. During the retreat however, we seemed weighed down with the hopelessness of it all. The Germans were men like ourselves and of course felt the same.

Whatever the cause, we made great strides in the summer and captured many prisoners. Too many really. Our Colonel said one night, before a dawn attack, "I am not telling you to kill your prisoners, but remember that they have to be fed, and out of your rations." As our rations were almost non-existent already, that was rich! He was not heartless, but his duty lay with his own troops. As we had been advancing rapidly our rations could not keep up with us, including our water in petrol cans, which gave a distinctive flavour to everything, especially tea, if there was a chance to make any.

On taking over Jerry's old lines, we found that many abandoned pieces of equipment had been booby-trapped. A favourite stunt. Even dead bodies were wired to explode when moved.

On my birthday, 10th September 1918, we had to drive the enemy from behind a railway embankment. From one of these, as I knew from my own machine gun experience, a few of their guns could traverse over a wide area holding up a whole regiment with little danger to themselves. Both sides made use of a type of Verey rocket which gave a bright light in order to see any movement of the enemy. On our side, three floating red lights, one above the other, was an SOS usually asking for artillery support. These were being sent up on that day and the big guns plastered the back of the embankment for a while. When that eased off, we went forward, took the objective, but lost quite a lot of men in doing it.

Breaking through the Hindenburg Line

Our division's biggest and, as it turned out most famous, job was the breaking of the impregnable Hindenburg Line constructed in the early days of the war. It stretched for miles and included the Scheldt Canal. This Line was reputed to be a veritable honeycomb of machine gun nests; and so we found it to be. Our objective was at a bend in the canal, at Bellenglise, which was said to be one of the toughest spots of all. Good old 46th Division.

The canal had at some points drained to a few feet owing to burst banks, but where we were going the water was about eight to ten feet deep. So during the night we were issued with lifebuoys stuffed with kapok. The idea was to part swim and part wade across, rifles held above the head, machine guns ditto. When you realised that the gun alone weighed over 90 pounds and Jerry would be firing at you all the time from the opposite bank, you could see what a picnic it would be. The other members of your team were loaded up with ammunition and a canvas bucket of Mills grenades. So, all set for a real good time.

At 5.20am on 29th September 1918, an enormous barrage opened up. It was tremendous. Everything possible was rained on the rear of the canal to prevent their reserves being brought up. The other side knew something was on by the intensity of our barrage, so up went their flares, green and gold, and over came the counter barrage. The racket was awe-inspiring. It was impossible to hear, even if orders were given. Over we went, slipping and sliding down the canal bank to the cold water below. The opposite bank was pitted with machine gun nests in tunnels dug into the 30 foot high sloping bank. How any of us even reached the water beats me, but a surprising number did. The water was up to our armpits, and holding that gun above my head was bad enough, without being machine gunned as well.

Clawing our way onto the bank we were underneath some of the machine guns, making it more difficult for them to hit us. So my team and many others threw Mills grenades into the tunnels nearest to us, whilst clinging for dear life to any scrap of projection on the bank. After all these years, I still don't know how we got away with it.

The Germans on top of the bank had obviously retreated, as there was no more firing from that quarter. Danger lay in an unknown number who could be hiding in the tunnels. These would fire at our backs when we moved on. The practice was to shout down the tunnel mouths to the occupants ordering them to throw out their weapons and come out. Some did, but ignoring the order meant a Mills thrown in, so in the end most surrendered. After the prisoners were sent back we had to check the tunnels. There had been no time to set booby traps, I'm glad to say.

The Hindenburg Line was a marvellous piece of

fortification. The bank was drilled with an amazing amount of skill into a complete underground fort. Wooden stairs, some 20 of them, led down to huge rooms, all supported by beams and struts. Wire bunks with blankets still on them stood by some of the walls. Quite a lot of personal belongings had been left in their hurried departure. In one very large chamber, which I thought must be officers' quarters, there were tables, chairs and a piano, all taken from French houses of course. Considering the conditions we had existed in for years, you can guess what we said. I found a pair of fine boots there and, as those I had were in a bad state, I put them on and left mine. I wore those boots for the remainder of my service abroad and so busy were we that no officer told me off for wearing non-regulation boots.

We stopped beside the canal for one day. The 32nd Division leapfrogged through and carried on chasing the retreating Germans. Our Brigade Commander gave us a speech in a quiet spell, patting us on the back as one might say. "You boys have made history," he said. "Your deed today will never be forgotten." I wonder.

I was 19 years and three weeks old then. Near Bellenglise, marking the spot, there is now a memorial to our chaps who died in the crossing.

Promotion under fire

Peronne, held undisturbed by the Germans through the war, had obviously been a nice town but, being near to where we had crossed, the damage to it had of course been caused by our barrage.

One of the things we found in Peronne was a house which had been occupied, I should think by senior officers,

La Baraque British cemetery, 2.5 kilometres north east of Bellenglise

Courtesy of Brent Whittham and Terry Heard of www.ww1cemeteries.com

who had departed in a great hurry. We were warned not to enter or touch anything until it had been checked for booby-traps, which was a good warning because there were indeed some. The place was beautifully furnished and in the dining room a meal, breakfast I presumed, was laid. Quite a sumptuous 'do' it was too. On examination, everything on the table was wired to explosives. You would only have to lift a plate and, 'whoosh', up you would go. That was not the only instance - Jerry was good at it. Wonderfully ingenious people they were, that's why they took some beating.

One of their stunts was to connect the handle of a farm water pump to a mine, knowing we would need water. As mechanics they were wonderful.

By three o'clock on that day, 29th September 1918, we were three miles the other side of their Hindenburg Line, heading for Le Cateau, our next objective. The Germans did not put up the same resistance now. They were dispirited and in some cases gave themselves up directly we approached.

Le Cateau, however, was different. They were determined to make a stand there. We attacked at dawn on a very misty morning and had a rough time, losing more men than at the Hindenburg Line. The official casualty figure for that battle was eight hundred. By nightfall we had rooted them out, capturing more than one hundred machine guns and more prisoners than we knew what to do with. The 6th and 1st Divisions were, I think, on our left and they also reached their objective. The 13th British Division and the 2nd American Corps were forging ahead near us. The fight surrounding Le Cateau was more like early days; very severe, and our losses were terrible.

We managed with great loss to get across some pontoon bridges which the engineers and pioneers had miraculously rigged up overnight. We cleared some trenches there with bayonets and grenades, taking more prisoners, mostly boys younger than me. In front of us, across a flat area, was a ridge which erupted with tremendous machine gun fire as we approached. All our officers were killed in getting to that ridge and, by the time we reached its shelter, all NCOs but myself and another corporal were either dead or wounded. My team, now only myself and three others, set up our gun on top of the ridge, keeping our heads well down. Suddenly, lines of grey figures swarmed over towards the ridge. They were putting up a counter attack. I opened up with my gun, traversing left and right over the plain. I could actually see the men falling like nine-pins under my machine gun and others', but still they came on, reinforced by more and more waves of field grey. I thought we had had it. I felt a tap on my shoulder. It was our only surviving officer, a boy of my own age, a second lieutenant. He said "Corporal, as you are the senior NCO, you take sergeant. There is another corporal at the other end of the ridge."

So, there I was, made sergeant in the middle of a battle, all of us looking like finishing any minute, and most likely never to have the opportunity to wear the darned chevrons anyway.

Wounded in battle

On the 17th October 1918 we were in a location east of Bohain when suddenly firing started to come from the side of our position, then almost at the back of us. It didn't need brains to know what that meant. We were a few men, on a bit of a hill, being gradually surrounded. We hadn't a hope in hell of getting out of it. We kept up our fire and our artillery opened out on the rear of the German hordes, but it was too late, no one could get to us in time to help. I tried to edge along to the Lieutenant, 50 yards away, leaving my number two firing the gun, to ask if he agreed to us trying to crawl back before the encirclement was complete. Suddenly it seemed as though I had been kicked by a horse on the left knee. It gave way and I went rolling down the bank. All I could think of then was to get out of there before the only gap in the circle closed. I crawled, dragging that blasted leg, in between hundreds of our dead towards what I hoped was the right direction. I was more scared then than when I was behind my gun. So helpless. Even then, Jerry had to give me a parting gift: a bullet in the hip. I don't think he liked me!

After that I concluded that I had got away as there were no more shots coming my way. As I found out later, I crawled three miles before finding a First Aid post in a shell hole. On the way I had met a man from the 5th Sherwoods who had one eye shot out. We were both bleeding like hell but there wasn't time to think about it. We crawled along together, coming across an officer lying in a hole, groaning. He had been shot through a lung and had struggled so far before giving up. Poor devil, every time he breathed, blood and foam bubbled from holes in his chest. There was no hope for him, nothing we could do. He asked for water. I still had some in my water bottle and gave him this to keep. He asked me to take his wallet and identity discs. We stopped with him until he died and his last words were to thank us. What for, poor chap, I don't know. We couldn't do anything for him.

The chap at the First Aid post strapped up my knee and bound my thigh. He put a bandage around my mate's eye; he could not do much else to that. An ambulance eventually took us back to the 5th Casualty Clearing Station where we were treated by a doctor and a nurse, the first woman we had seen for months. She looked like an angel to us.

Back to Blighty

So I was last wounded on 17th October 1918, during the middle or at the end of one of the toughest spots I had been in with the Sherwoods. This was my last action in a battle of the First World War and it ended my active service career.

On 18th October 1918, we were moved to the base hospital (9th General Hospital) at Rouen, where I stopped for two days. Wounds or not, it was lovely to lie in a bed for the first time in months.

One of the doctors was American and, on what was known as 'marking out day', he was on duty. He had to give us a final examination to decide whether we could be sent to hospital at Etaples to be patched up for more service, or were serious enough to be sent back to Blighty. He would come along the line of beds and mark our case cards either 'E' for Etaples, or 'UK' for Britain. You can guess the tension in the wards. When he had gone, we had to ask the nurse what was marked on our cards. I was almost afraid to ask, but when I did, it was 'UK'.

After two days in Rouen, I was then taken by hospital train to Le Havre for a ship to Britain. I had lost sight of my mate with the eye injury and never saw him again. We wounded were loaded onto the hospital ship *Aberdonian* on the night of 22nd October 1918, and taken to Southampton. Although I was going back to my home country, I felt more scared of torpedoes as we zigzagged across the Channel because I was in bed below decks and felt so helpless. I don't know that one had more hope on deck, but that was the general feeling. Just to make things worse, the sea was very choppy. Darn it though, we were going home!

As we entered Southampton harbour, it was pitch black. We stretcher cases were unloaded onto the docks and lay there in rows. Red Cross girls and other volunteers brought us tea or coffee and smokes. We were also given a handkerchief each, embroidered with a red cross in the corner. An RAMC officer and a transport officer sorted out where we were to go and, of course, home being in the south east, I was sent to the west in the usual army style. It turned out to be to the Beaufort War Hospital in the Fishponds district of Bristol. In peacetime this was a mental hospital and, owing to overcrowding, myself and a few others were put singly in padded cells. We had plenty of leg-pulling over that.

Recuperation at Longleat

I stayed there until 6th November 1918, when I was transferred to hospital at a beautiful spot near Warminster in Wiltshire. This was Longleat, the huge country home of the Marquess of Bath who had given over a wing of the house for use as a Red Cross VAD Hospital. A very lovely Elizabethan house surrounded by its own large park in which red deer roamed. Certainly heaven to us after the battlefields. We were welcomed by the Lady Kathleen, elder daughter of the Marquess who, as a high ranking officer in the Red Cross Society, was helping to run it. Four of us were put in a room on the west side of the house and we all became great pals. The nurses and everyone were most kind. I shall always remember Longleat with gratitude. It seemed like a dream, to be suddenly wafted from all that horror to a nice bed and peaceful nights.

On the morning of 10th November 1918, we on the first floor heard a terrific din coming from the lower part of the house. We were told that an Armistice had been signed and the war was over. Gongs were sounding, kitchen pots banged, everything that would make a row. Then the shock. We were told that the news was too previous; it was not over. Such was the let-down that when the Armistice was signed the next day, 11th November 1918, we didn't believe it at first. So there it was. After all the death and suffering, I only wish that the high hopes we all had then for future peace had been realised.

Later in my time at Longleat, when the weather permitted, the others and I were taken out on the lawns by nurses. My knee had been operated on during the first week I was there and eventually I was able to get myself about in a self-propelled chair. I became quite expert at getting down long corridors, around the wards, and later around the park, which I was told was some seven miles. There was one long path called the Rhododendron Walk. It must have been a picture at flowering time, which was not when I was there.

Lord Bath and his staff had one of the huge barns fitted up as a theatre and his family and the staff took part in short plays. I participated on two or three occasions as a wounded cavalier, complete with shoulder length dark curls and a beautiful period costume. Once I was a shy but beautiful girl, also with long dark curls. I was often told what a fine girl I made, and you can guess what rather rude offers I had from my mates, being soldiers! I'm afraid I do not make such a fine girl now, better for an old lady's part.

There was one occasion when one of our chaps had to go to the dentist, the nearest being at Frome, not far from Longleat. By then I was managing to get about with a stick and Lady Kathleen asked if I would like to take him there in one of their pony carts. It would be a change for me, she said. It was! I didn't like to admit that I had never handled a horse but, being brought up to ride from childhood herself, she took it for granted. I got the pony started and off down the Rhododendron Walk we went. He was a nice docile creature and bowled along happily. I would have enjoyed it

Convalescing servicemen on the front steps of Longleat House in 1916. Courtesy of Longleat House.

71

more if I had been sure how to stop him at journey's end. However, he stopped first time. No doubt he had been there lots of times. Going back was fine: I had confidence in the horse and he knew his way without me.

I was sorry to leave Longleat - they were good kind folks with nothing snobbish about them. The Marchioness spent the last years of her life lying flat in a spinal carriage. I think she was injured in a hunting accident but I am not sure. We often saw her. I remember her as a very aristocratic looking lady with a pale face.

Christmas at West Hall

My next abode was a so-called convalescent camp near Sunderland. The army had taken over a very ancient manor house called West Hall, at Whitburn. It was at the end of a long drive, with trees meeting overhead making it very dark. There were signs of great neglect. The ballroom was used as the canteen; a large room with gilded cornices and pillars. It must have been lovely in better days. Half a dozen of us were put in the various rooms. There was an atmosphere about the place which gave me a creepy feeling, and one night it came to a head. We were all asleep, it must have been the early hours of the morning, when someone screamed in a room next to us. There was a lot of shouting and we all went into the corridor to see what was going on. The fellows in that room said that something had walked across their room screaming and the blankets were tugged off their beds. "It was a misty sort of figure," said those who saw it. Well, not much sleep that night! Next morning that room was boarded up and not used again. Later, we were told in the village that it had been the scene of terrible happenings during the Civil War and had not been occupied for years owing to the haunting. Trust the army to keep it quiet. Just to help things, one of our chaps hanged himself from a tree in the avenue the next day.

I spent Christmas at West Hall where the old conservatory was set out with tables and decorated with paper-chains and holly. It was the first Christmas away from the fighting for most of us. In the traditional way, the officers waited on us. We had turkey, pudding, wine and rum and it was a nice happy 'do'. At the end, the colonel gave a short speech in which he said how proud he was to have fought beside the finest amateur soldiers one could wish for. He, like all of us, was waiting for his discharge. Everybody was happy. We certainly were a fine body of men: some hobbling on sticks like me, some with crutches. We couldn't do any duties except peel spuds, so time dragged badly.

One of the colliery owners thought some of us would like to see inside a mine. I had a horror of heights and being closed in but didn't like to refuse what was meant to be a kind gesture. So a few of us went. The cage, that is a sort of lift which takes the miners down to the pit, looked an awful shaky thing to us, no sides to it, just a loose rail. When it took us down, it wobbled from side to side. Quite honestly I hated it. The pit itself was a series of low roofed tunnels, all black and smelling of musty airlessness. We were only taken a short way as we cripples found it difficult to get over the rough floor. I think that I was not the only one glad to see daylight and smell the fresh air again. Of course a great number of my fellow Sherwoods were miners in civvy life. They didn't bother to go down. Why should they?

I was at West Hall until 2nd February 1919. I and a

number of others were called to the CO's office one day and told that we had a choice. We wounded were waiting in the usual way for the disability pension people to sort us out with our grades of disablement. I was graded C2. It might take months more but, and here lay the cunning, if we signed a paper called Form Z22 in which we would agree to accept whatever pension they awarded, we could be discharged at once. I was still young, so like others I signed it. A great number of us have been sorry since, but it is no good regretting that now.

The Crystal Palace and home

We who came from the south were given rail warrants for London. So, in the charge of a sergeant major who was also being discharged, we said "cheerio" to all our pals who were going in other directions and boarded the train for the south. This was the last time that I went anywhere under the command of a sergeant major.

Our immediate destination was Penge for the Crystal Palace which I think had been occupied by the naval authorities during the war but was now used as a dispersal centre for troops being discharged. As I have already mentioned, I had visited the Palace when I was a boy, as a member of one of the school choirs which competed each year at the Empire Singing Festival. I went several years running and it was a wonderful affair. Ah, happy days when being kids you do not know what is in front of you.

When we arrived this time, tables had been placed at intervals around the long metal-latticed galleries, and we were interviewed and given a form at each table. After visiting all the tables you had quite a sheaf of them, among them the discharge papers. I, with a few chaps who were going my way, left the Palace at about 1.00am and caught one of the extra trains to Victoria Station running for troops going home, then the train to Brighton. The first time home for ten months.

I arrived at 74 Hanover Terrace at 2.30am. Of course they were all asleep. Selfishly I suppose, I knocked and knocked, until Dad's voice called to know who was there. I shouted through the letterbox, "It's George!" Mum and Dad tumbled out of bed and down the stairs, and what a welcome I had. Poor old Mum said "I am so very glad you are safe," and hugged me. Dad was not usually one to show his feelings, but even he was nearly in tears. Yes, it's nice to be wanted!

We were all drinking tea for a couple of hours before trying to get a bit of sleep. Then up in the bedroom my brothers wanted to know all about my adventures, so I doubt whether we had much rest that night.

Ahead of me now was the settling down to civilian life as a man. I had left it as an inexperienced boy.

We had been dished out with some pretty awful demob suits at the Palace but having grown and developed in the years, none of my pre-war clothes would fit so until I could get others, even that was useful. My uniform with its sergeant's chevrons earned on the battlefield and hardly worn was put away for good.

And that is the end of the tale of a boy swaddy.

Postscript

Soon after demobilisation, George Parker rejoined the Co-op at their branch in North Road, Brighton where he met and fell in love with Ivy Kingsley.

In the early days of the 1920s and the Depression, George found himself unemployed alongside thousands of others. He attempted to rejoin the Army but was considered unfit due to his war injuries. Eventually finding work with the Co-op in Haywards Heath, he took lodgings with a family friend in the unspoilt village of Lindfield. He was very happy there and, not yet married, he and Ivy would meet at weekends.

When offered a job in a Brighton grocers, he moved back there to be closer to her, only to find himself out of work again a year later, whereupon he became a travelling salesman for a cloth merchants until the outbreak of the Second World War. For many years, he had been an active member of the British Red Cross Society and he signed up with them as a full-time volunteer.

George and Ivy married at Dorset Gardens Church in 1927, but sadly Ivy died from tubercular illness aged 25 only seven weeks after giving birth to their daughter, Patricia, in March 1929.

George died in 1973 a year after this photograph was taken.